NEW INTERPRETATIONS IN AMERICAN FOREIGN POLICY

By ALEXANDER DECONDE

The University of California, Santa Barbara

COMMITTEE ON

TEACHING OF THE

AMERICAN HISTORICAL

ASSOCIATION

PREFACE

A few words on the philosophy and structure of this pamphlet seem appropriate in this new edition. This pamphlet remains essentially an essay on some broad trends in interpretations followed by brief specific summaries of the interpretations or contributions in individual works. For this subject this approach has appeared more useful to the teacher than a long essay on interpretations supported by bibliographical citations.

Although some significant works on American diplomatic history have been published recently in foreign languages, they have not in general offered important new interpretations and they are difficult for the teacher to obtain. This study, therefore, has been confined mainly to works in English available to the teacher in most major libraries.

As can be seen from a quick perusal of the contents, not even all the recent books in English on foreign policy are discussed. The offerings, in other words, are selected ones. I hope my choices are judicious, but if any reader believes that I have omitted important works that should be included, I shall be grateful if he would bring such books or articles, or any other suggestion for improvement, to my attention.

Lastly, I must mention that because of limitations of space I have restricted my analysis mainly to the flood of new books on foreign policy and have not been able to give as much attention to the periodical literature as it merits.

ALEXANDER DeConde

Ann Arbor, Michigan

New Interpretations in American Foreign Policy

By ALEXANDER DECONDE

THE SCOPE OF THIS PAMPHLET

Historians agree that it takes a long time for new interpretations in American history to reach and find acceptance by the general public, by the college and secondary school textbooks, and by the teachers of history and social science in the secondary schools. Some historians have estimated it takes about twenty years, so this pamphlet will review and explain some of the changes in the writing and teaching of the history of American foreign policy in the past quarter of a century. It will also review, summarize, and explain some of the new interpretations or contributions that have appeared in the literature of American diplomatic history in those years.

SOURCES OF CHANGING INTERPRETATIONS

Until recently the historians and others who have written on the history of American foreign policy have generally been more factual and less theoretical than those in other fields of American history. No historian of American foreign policy has produced a sweeping interpretation comparable to Frederick Jackson Turner's frontier thesis and its influence on American development or any theory comparable to Alfred Thayer Mahan's on the influence of sea power on history. American diplomatic historians have not advanced new large interpretations that have upset accepted views. So we may conclude that broad theories or theses in the past two and a half decades have not greatly influenced the writing or teaching of American diplomatic history.

The diplomatic historian has usually restricted himself to cautious partial interpretations and has advanced them as provisional hypotheses. Most of his interpretations have not been concerned with over-all perspective. They have been restricted and limited to special circumstances and have been more controversial than "new." Yet, there have been enough changes in interpretations of American diplomatic history to give new understanding and enlarged perspective in explaining America's foreign policies. Some critics have pointed out that historians of foreign policy have too often stayed close to the surface of events by presenting mere digests of official correspondence in some connected form without adequately explaining underlying economic and social forces, motives, and basic assumptions. The diplomatic historian, they have argued, has been unwilling to interpret far enough beyond his documents to explain how foreign policy came to be what it was.

True enough, trained historians have been wary, and understandably so, of hasty generalization and broad interpretation in a field so complex as that of American foreign policy.

Today, however, the better diplomatic historian presents his facts and conclusions so as to show clearly what his generalizations mean. He examines his assumptions and interprets his findings so that they will test existing interpretations and raise new questions. Sometimes those findings will produce new interpretations.

Along with their critics, American diplomatic historians have recognized that foreign policy, especially in the twentieth century, is not restricted to the relations between the foreign offices of governments. In recent years the history of American foreign policy has covered a wider area than ever before. The line between domestic and foreign affairs has blurred.

The American government, for one thing, has engaged in activities that until recently belonged to private citizens and private organizations. It has discussed problems with foreign governments that ranged from tariffs on bicycles to the immigration and feeding of political refugees. Those who write and those who teach American diplomatic history have had to try to explain how those problems influenced foreign policy. To do that they have often had to go outside the traditional demarcations of diplomatic history. They have had to venture into such fields as economics, public administration, social institutions, the psychology of race relations, and space exploration.

The history of American foreign policy, even more than that of other special areas of America's development, has been enriched and influenced by the growing trend to interpret the American past within the whole context of Western civilization. Special historical theories, often carried over from other disciplines such as philosophy, political science, sociology, psychology, and economics, have influenced the enlarged scope of the history of American foreign policy.

PUBLIC OPINION, IDEAS, AND IDEOLOGIES

Students of American foreign policy in the past two and a half decades have also been increasingly concerned with the impact of public opinion, of domestic politics, and of pressure groups on developments in foreign policy. They have had to evaluate the elements of mass opinion which in recent years have increasingly helped to form policy at home and abroad. They have had to try to measure deflections in foreign policy caused by particular interest and pressure groups, and have had to be aware of oversimplified issues raised by politicians or forced on statesmen by the electorate.

Since government documents in matters of mass opinion have limitations, the historian of foreign policy has had to supplement his documents with other sources. He has had to deal with ideas and ideologies, with the power of racial, social, and religious prejudices, and with the media of mass communications that now influence foreign policy. The press, radio, and television are now more and more interested in foreign policy, and they help to mold mass opinion. Since the newspapers and their columnists are increasingly concerned with international developments, they have in recent years given wide news coverage to foreign affairs. The columnists have interpreted foreign policy as it was made and so have popular writers whose books on diplomacy have reached the public in ever larger numbers. The diplomatic historian has to take all these developments into account and to try to measure their influence on foreign policy.

The recent rise of American intellectual history in the universities has also had a fertilizing effect on the study of diplomatic history and of America's role in international politics. The diplomatic historian, as a result, has shown a new concern for ideas in foriegn policy. He now wants to know what Americans thought about their foreign policy almost as much as he wants to know about foreign policy itself. Conflicts in foreign policy, when viewed in the context of the emotional and intellectual traditions they expressed, he knows, appear better rounded and in clearer perspective than when isolated.

The Emphasis on Military Power, Science and Technology

In the past twenty-five years the historian of foreign policy has had to take into account, more than in the past, the influence of military theory and power on foreign policy and international politics. Earlier, American diplomatic historians frequently ignored military power, even though it has always been an essential ingredient in world politics. If historians do not consider American military resources, especially when dealing with the events of the twentieth century, they cannot explain and interpret the workings of foreign policy, even though they might follow the development of diplomacy carefully and accurately through its proper historical institutions. Now diplomatic historians must also explore, as political scientists are doing, the great issues raised by the impact of scientific and technological change on the issues of war and peace, on foreign policy, and on international affairs in general. Nuclear weapons and space missiles, they must understand, can suddenly change the balance of power among nations and alter basic principles in the conduct of American foreign policy.

The student of American foreign policy has always been aware of the large part that all forms of physical power have played in international politics. But in recent years he has tried increasingly to answer the question, did the United States in its foreign policy act solely in terms of power or on the basis of other considerations, such as ethical principles? Although power has always been a fundamental element in American foreign policy and the diplomatic historian has never disregarded it, he has not generally considered it as the only source of action. Recent interpretations have placed it in a perspective of "right" and "wrong" policy. Sometimes the historian has been unable to disentangle it from those considerations.

CAUSES OF CONTROVERSY

One form of interpretation that has never been lacking in the history of American foreign policy is that dealing with underlying causes and motivation. While almost all historians have disagreed most often and most vehemently on cause and motivation, the disagreements of American historians over recent foreign policy on these points have been particularly bitter. One reason for this is that historical objectivity may not be more than a noble dream that seldom becomes real. So there will always be changing interpretations, and those interpretations will often be subjective and controversial. Another reason for controversy is that recent American foreign policy has been a matter of almost universal concern. It has directly affected the lives of more Americans than at any time in the past. Diplomatic historians in their writings, therefore, could hardly avoid hot disagreement.

That disagreement has touched the basic philosophies of history and the very nature of history itself. It has shown to many that the facts do not speak for themselves. In one way or another the historian interprets them. In the sciences and in other disciplines experts have also disagreed and do disagree on fundamental interpretations, but they have seldom disagreed with the rancor and far-reaching public effect with which American historians of foreign policy have in recent years. The disagreements of the diplomatic historians on matters of interpretation, as to the causes for American entrance in the two world wars or the soundness of American policy toward China in the 1940's, for instance, have reached the public. Moreover, they have influenced the public and the political reaction to foreign policy.

PRESENT SCHOLARSHIP: INTERPRETATION AND THE SOURCES

Since the history of American foreign policy in recent years has widened in scope, taking into consideration diverse internal developments as well as enlarged questions of international politics, it has become one of the more complex special fields of American historical scholarship.

Most diplomatic historians have been concerned with the new vastness and richness of their sources. Those sources, multiplied by America's increasing intercourse with other nations, have practically overwhelmed them. So they have marked off their work into smaller and smaller areas of investigation. So detailed and so lacking in connection to the main currents of American development have many of their monographs been that few could be used meaningfully by the high school student of average intelligence. Until the past several decades, in fact, not even the average college undergraduate read many of those monographs in his history courses. In many universities, moreover, the work in American diplomatic history was restricted to the graduate level.

Probably no historian can write on the history of American foreign policy in the traditional manner from the sources and scattered archives and still produce a book with broad perspective. One lifetime may be too short. The limited monographs and the heavily documented articles in the professional magazines, therefore, continue to form the backbone of scholarship in the history of American foreign policy. They contain the latest thinking, the new information, and the significant, if limited, interpretations. The better teacher, therefore, will want to know the monographic literature and from it usually make his own broad interpretations.

The Textbooks

Before discussing some of the specific new interpretations and partial interpretations taken from recent monographic and general literature on the history of American foreign policy, we should take note of the textbooks on American diplomatic history used currently in the colleges and universities. Depending on the date of the latest complete revision, they contain the major new interpretations taken from the more specialized sources.

Samuel F. Bemis' *A Diplomatic History of the United States* is a book of careful scholarship written from "a multi-archival approach." The author believes that American diplomatic history must come from the archives and sources of all the governments with whom the United States has relations and this book represents his enlarged international approach to that history. Bemis tries "to give perspective and interpretation to the whole diplomatic history and foreign policy of the United States." The book first appeared in 1936 and is now in its fourth edition, published in 1955. A condensed version, entitled *A Short History of American Foreign Policy and Diplomacy,* appeared in 1959.

In 1940 Thomas A. Bailey published *A Diplomatic History of the American People.* Since then the book has gone through six editions, the last one a complete revision published in 1958, to become the most widely read text in American diplomatic history. The title reflects the book's theme, mainly the influence of public opinion, or of the people, on foreign policy. Bailey believes that diplomatic affairs cannot be conducted in a vacuum "isolated from political, economic, and social developments," so he placed the history of American foreign policy in a broad setting and at the same time stressed personalities. The book reflects the trend of viewing diplomatic history in a larger context, is scholarly and unusually readable. Its first five editions are also valuable for their extensive bibliographies covering the latest literature in the field. Many titles include concise explanations of the newest interpretations.

Another departure from the traditional pattern of diplomatic history is Richard W. Van Alstyne's *American Diplomacy in Action,* published in 1944, and in a second edition in 1947. In 1952 Van Alstyne supplemented it with *American Crisis Diplomacy: The Quest for Collective Security, 1918–1952.* In his text he has put aside the chronological approach and has interpreted American diplomatic history as a series of related instances or cases. He has applied, in effect, the case study method of the lawyer to the study of American foreign policy, an approach that reflects the force of outside influences on the study of American diplomatic history.

L. Ethan Ellis, in *A Short History of American Diplomacy,* published in 1951, also departed from the usual chronological treatment. He interpreted the history of American foreign policy under a broad topical arrangement that concentrated on major issues and developments. He made his interpretation a "working tool for understanding the main forces which shape American foreign policy and the chief avenues which that policy has followed."

A few years later, in 1955, Julius W. Pratt published *A History of United States Foreign Policy*. This book follows the traditional chronological pattern and interprets the history of American foreign policy as an integrated story with explanations of principles woven into the narrative. The author takes a broad view of diplomatic history, one that stresses the enlarged importance of military power as "an indispensable instrument in the prosecution of foreign policy." He also reflects the latest interpretations on the aims of foreign policy by giving attention to such concepts as "ideals and self-interest."

Robert H. Ferrell's new text, *American Diplomacy: A History* (1959), is relatively short. It saves space by offering a brief statement of events prior to the 1890's and emphasizing the diplomacy of the twentieth century. Like Ellis' book, it takes certain topics, such as relations with Latin America, and treats them as units. Hence, it does not follow a strictly chronological pattern. This book is distinguished by clear writing and provocative analyses that accompany the basic narrative.

The newest text, Jules Davids' *America and the World of Our Time: United States Diplomacy in the Twentieth Century* (1960), is a specialized book, one that deals exclusively with the diplomacy of the twentieth century. Davids' purpose is to present American foreign policy in a world context, which he attempts to do by treating selected topics, particularly by stressing America's involvement in power politics, changes in foreign policy brought about by the Second World War, and the diplomatic background of the cold war.

COLONIAL, REVOLUTIONARY, AND FEDERALIST PERIODS

Max Savelle has written a number of articles tracing the beginnings of American diplomatic history in the colonial period. In "The American Balance of Power and European Diplomacy, 1713–78" (see Richard B. Morris [ed.], *The Era of the American Revolution* [1939], pp. 140–169), he re-emphasizes the theme that France aided the United States and conceived the alliance of 1778 in self-interest. France, he shows, supported the American Revolution to create a balance of power in the western hemisphere as well as in Europe.

Felix Gilbert, in "The English Background of American Isolationism in the Eighteenth Century" (see *The William and Mary Quarterly*, I, Third Series [April, 1944], 138-160), interprets the beginnings of American isolationism as stemming from England. Benjamin Franklin, Thomas Paine, and others, he says, brought isolationist sentiments and ideas to America. In his pamphlet, *Common Sense*, Paine recommended political isolation from Europe. Gilbert believes that Paine's ideas influenced George Washington's Farewell Address, Federalist foreign policy, and Thomas Jefferson's foreign policy.

Gerald Stourzh, in *Benjamin Franklin and American Foreign Policy* (1954), has written one of the few books that combine the history of ideas with foreign policy. He has concentrated on motives underlying political action and has analyzed "Franklin's approach to foreign policy by probing his actions as well as his expression of opinion concerning international politics." He interprets Franklin's ideas on foreign policy in terms of power politics and enlightened self-interest. Franklin's concept of foreign policy, according to Stourzh's interpretation, was "based on his all-powerful desire of living space for a rapidly increasing people." This book brings something of a fresh approach to the study of the history of American foreign policy.

Following the traditional approach of concentrating on a close use of diplomatic correspondence, Arthur Burr Darling, in *Our Rising Empire, 1763-1803* (1940), wrote a detailed history of American foreign policy in the Revolutionary and Federalist eras, focusing his attention on American efforts to obtain the Mississippi Valley. He stressed two main themes. No one of the great powers of the time, Great Britain, France or Spain, he explained, wished to see the United States establish itself in the valley. Secondly, the men who guided American foreign policy had a vision of empire, and in seeking territorial gains they displayed as much hard political realism as did their European antagonists.

While emphasizing diplomacy, Alexander DeConde, in *Entangling Alliance: Politics and Diplomacy under George Washington* (1958), has written a synthesis showing the interaction of ideas, politics and foreign policy during Washington's administrations. His main theme is the combined influence of diplomacy and domestic politics on the French alliance of 1778. In analyzing the origin of national political parties, he presented the thesis that differences over foreign policy contributed to the formation of parties because foreign policy touched on national issues and transcended sectional differences. Louis Martin Sears, in *George Washington and the French Revolution* (1960), advanced a similar thesis.

In foreign policy, DeConde challenged the traditional interpretation of the Federalist era as being the golden age of American diplomacy and "the classic age of American statecraft." He pointed out that the statesmen of the Washington period often played their politics and diplomacy by ear and sometimes placed political advantage above national welfare. In their struggles over foreign policy, the Federalists and Republicans were motivated by their own self-interests. He also contended that the Washigton era was not essentially isolationist and that it did not truly set a precedent for isolationism. In his view, the American attitude toward Europe and isolationism was mixed. Some Americans were isolationists and some wanted their government to take part in the international politics of Europe.

ANGLO-AMERICAN RELATIONS

Bradford Perkins, in *The First Rapprochement: England and the United States, 1795–1805* (1955), shows that capable diplomacy, particularly on the part of England, made possible the first Anglo-American understanding after the hostility bred by the American Revolution. Events after 1805 that destroyed the accord he blames on inept diplomacy by both sides. With qualification, he attributes most of the fault to the Jeffersonian Republicans who later led the nation into the War of 1812.

In another study of events leading to that war, "George Canning, Great Britain, and the United States, 1807–1809" (see *The American Historical Review*, LXIII [October, 1957], 1–22), Perkins suggests that contrary to earlier interpretations, Canning, the British Foreign Secretary, was not blindly anti-American and points out that Canning and his colleagues "never completely lost sight of the advantages of American neutrality." Under Canning's leadership Great Britain even made several conciliatory gestures toward the United States, he writes, concessions that failed because the British statesmen misunderstood the Americans and underestimated America's strength.

When Alfred L. Burt published *The United States, Great Britain, and British North America: From the Revolution to the Establishment of Peace After the War of 1812* (1940), he challenged a number of existing interpretations about our early relations with Great Britain. His interpretation of the diplomacy leading to the Jay Treaty of 1794 differs from that of Samuel F. Bemis in his *Jay's Treaty* (1923). Burt argues that the United States could not have wrung concessions from Great Britain in its war with France even if John Jay had threatened to bring the United States into the Armed Neutrality of the northern European nations and had not been undercut by Alexander Hamilton, who told the Birtish the United States would not join the armed neutrals.

Burt also rejects the traditional American view that Great Britain held the northwest posts after 1783, in violation of the peace treaty, because Great Britain wanted to continue its monopoly of the fur trade. That interpretation, he says, is based on "national suspicion and prejudice." According to his interpretation, the British held on to the posts indefinitely primarily because they had blundered in neglecting the welfare of the Indians in the peace treaty of 1783 and because of "American weakness." After the peace Great Britain tried to rectify the "blunder" by protecting the Indians against the Americans and in so doing retained the posts.

When dealing with the causes of the War of 1812 Burt again rejects generally accepted interpretations. He argues in particular against the thesis of Julius W. Pratt, expressed in his *Expansionists of 1812* (1925), that without the ambitions of aggressive westerners and their grievances against Great Britain there would have been no war. He re-emphasizes, instead, the older interpretations of the war as one for free trade and sailors' rights. "The impressment issue," he concludes, "was the rock that wrecked the last hope of peace."

In his interpretation of the war causes Burt has revised a revision. He has illustrated how historical interpretations sometimes work in cycles, and how interpretation in history is linked to the subjective appraisal of the historian himself. This can be seen in Warren H. Goodman, "The Origins of the War of 1812: A Survey of Changing Interpretations" (see *The Mississippi Valley Historical Review*, XXVIII [September, 1941], 171– 186). The author has reviewed the literature on the causes of the War of 1812 and, like Burt, maintains that the maritime factors deserve more consideration in interpreting the causes of the war than the Pratt thesis gives them.

Concentrating on the creation, development and decline of an Anglo-American community of economics and ideas in the first half of the nineteenth century, Frank Thistlethwaite, in *The Anglo-American Connection in the Early Nineteenth Century* (1959), does not deal with conventional foreign relations. Instead, he has written a book on the transit of ideas across international boundaries. His thesis states that the complementary nature of the British and American economies disappeared as that of the United States matured from a "colonial" to a "metropolitan" economy, a change completed by the end of the Civil War when the economic connection between the two countries lost its unique character.

Charles P. Stacey, in "The Myth of the Unguarded Frontier, 1815–1871" (see *The American Historical Review*, LVI [October, 1950], 1–18), corrects earlier interpretations of the significance of the Rush-Bagot Agreement of 1817. He explains that the "undefended border" between the United States and Canada dates from the Washington Treaty of 1871, not from the agreement of 1817 which was limited to naval disarmament on the Great Lakes and Lake Champlain. His evidence shows that the idea of the "unfortified frontier" is founded on legend. The earlier interpretation is summarized by Edgar W. McInnis in *The Unguarded Frontier: A History of American-Canadian Relations* (1942), p. 146.

Charles S. Campbell's *Anglo-American Understanding, 1898–1903* (1957) stresses that the threat of war between the United States and Britain over a boundary in Venezuela in 1896, the

Spanish-American and the Boer wars were essential factors in bringing about the Anglo-American rapprochement at the turn of the century. By pointing out that patient negotiations between the United States and Britain—discussions that sometimes included Canada—were necessary for the good understanding. Campbell advances the idea that diplomacy made it possible.

In the first comprehensive survey of Anglo-American relations since the 1920's, Henry C. Allen, in *Great Britain and the United States: A History of Anglo-American Relations, 1783–1952* (1955), concentrates on the friendship between the two countries and the shift in the balance of power between the two. "My object," he says in explaining his theme, "has been to tell the story of the Anglo-American relationship in the past in order that we may the better guide its course in the future." Unlike Campbell, he sees the beginnings, at least, of the Anglo-American bond in the 1850's rather than the 1890's.

THE ERA OF MONROE

Recent studies have placed the treaty of February 22, 1819, with Spain in a larger context than did past interpretations. Scholars no longer refer to it merely as the Florida treaty; they recognize that it was much broader and that it solved other boundary problems in North America. Since the treaty brought the United States to the Pacific Ocean, through Spain's surrender of her claims to Oregon, Samuel F. Bemis has called it the "Transcontinental Treaty." His earlier writings placed the treaty in its larger setting, but he has brought his findings together in *John Quincy Adams and the Foundations of American Foreign Policy* (1949). Philip C. Brooks, in *Diplomacy and the Borderlands: The Adams-Onís Treaty of 1819* (1939), also placed the treaty in its broader context.

In 1936 Edward T. Tatum, Jr., in *The United States and Europe, 1815–1823: A Study in the Background of the Monroe Doctrine,* challenged the accepted interpretation that the Monroe Doctrine was aimed primarily against the Holy Alliance and France, and Russian expansion in North America. According to his interpretation, the menace of the Holy Alliance was an English invention and the Monroe Doctrine was directed against England and her designs on Cuba. Other historians of the Monroe Doctrine have not generally accepted this interpretation.

Dexter Perkins, in *A History of the Monroe Doctrine* (1955), a summary of his earlier researches, re-emphasizes the traditional interpretation. So does Arthur P. Whitaker, with some modification, in *The United States and the Independence of Latin America, 1800–1830* (1941). Gale W. McGee in "The Monroe Doctrine —A Stopgap Measure" (see *The Mississippi Valley Historical Review*, XXXVIII [September, 1951], 233–150), interprets the Monroe Doctrine as a temporary expedient, "a stopgap measure," designed to hold off European designs on the Americas while the United States negotiated with England over a joint declaration.

Expansion to the Pacific

Frederick Merk, in *Albert Gallatin and the Oregon Problem: A Study in Anglo-American Diplomay* (1950), throws new light on the non-colonization principle of the Monroe Doctrine. His thesis states that in the negotiations of 1826–27 with Great Britain over the Oregon country the United States followed a "containment policy." That policy expanded the non-colonization principle so as to check English and other European settlements in North America. "It was made," the author said, "the announced program of the United States in the Pacific Northwest."

Norman A. Graebner, in *Empire on the Pacific: A Study of American Continental Expansion* (1955), concludes that previous interpretations have overrated American settlement and "manifest destiny" as determining elements in American expansion into Oregon and California. His thesis insists that mercantile interests in the Pacific area "determined the course of empire," and that it was "through clearly conceived policies relentlessly pursued that the United States achieved its empire on the Pacific."

Analyzing political attitudes and the complex motives of international behavior, Albert K. Weinberg, in *Manifest Destiny: A Study of Nationalist Expansionism in American History* (1935), wrote the pioneering study on the ideology of expansion, one that linked ideas and social impulses to the shaping of foreign policy.

He sought to discover what reasoning led Americans to believe as they did and do as they did in their relations with other peoples. His thesis states that Americans justified expansion to promote a security that had already been established and to carry out their "manifest destiny" of bringing the political and social blessings of democracy to others.

Two men doing independent research on the same subject, neither aware of the researches of the other, recently corrected an erroneous interpretation of the place of expansion in the presidential election of 1844. Edwin A. Miles, a historian, in " 'Fifty-four Forty or Fight'—An American Political Legend," (see *The Mississippi Valley Historical Review*, XLIV [September, 1957], 291–309) and Hans Sperber, a professor of German, in " 'Fifty-four Forty or Fight': Facts and Fictions," (see *American Speech*, XXXII [February, 1957], 5–11), show that "Fifty-four forty or fight" was not a campaign slogan that virtually won the election for Polk and the Democratic party. The slogan, it is pointed out, was not used at all in the campaign and did not gain currency until one year after Polk's inauguration. Miles also advances the thesis that historians have hence overemphasized the role of Oregon in the election of 1844.

In another study of Anglo-American diplomacy in the western hemisphere, "British Diplomacy and the Clayton-Bulwer Treaty, 1850–1860" (see *The Journal of Modern History*, XI [June, 1939], 149–183), Richard W. Van Alstyne has interpreted the Clayton-Bulwer Treaty as *a permanent alliance* with England designed to effect a common settlement in central America. "It made the United States," he said, "an American power, equal in every respect to the only other first-class American power, Great Britain."

Anatole G. Mazour, in "The Prelude to Russia's Departure from America" (see *The Pacific Historical Review*, X [September, 1941], 311–319), dismisses the old thesis that Russia sold Alaska without knowing of its wealth "as sheer nonsense." He points out that the tsarist government knew of the gold there but sold Alaska anyway because it felt it might lose the province, because it was involved in other problems in Europe, and because it wanted to cultivate American friendship as a balance against England.

THE "NEW MANIFEST DESTINY"

Albert T. Volwiler, in "Harrison, Blaine, and American Foreign Policy, 1889–1893" (see *American Philosophical Society Proceedings*, LXXIX [1938], 637–648), advanced the thesis that the new imperialism began in the Benjamin Harrison administration. Julius W. Pratt, in *Expansionists of 1898* (1936), studied the "New Manifest Destiny" and analyzed the economic factors in it. He asked what was the "great cause" for the Spanish-American War? He refuted the idea that the United States fought for markets and fields for investment, and advanced the interpretation that American businessmen had consistently opposed action that would lead to war with Spain. They endorsed expansion only after the war began.

In *America's Colonial Experiment* (1950) Pratt analyzes American imperialism and concludes that on the whole it was benevolent. The United States, he says, embraced colonialism for political and strategic reasons; economic motives were less important.

William E. Leuchtenburg, in "Progressivism and Imperialism: The Progressive Movement and American Foreign Policy, 1898–1916" (see *The Mississippi Valley Historical Review*, XXXIX [December, 1952], 438–504), attempts to bridge the gulf between domestic and foreign affairs. His thesis suggests that Progressivism, contrary to past interpretations, did not oppose the new imperialism, but instead generally supported it.

Richard Hofstadter, in "Manifest Destiny and the Philippines" (see Daniel Aaron [ed.], *America in Crisis: Fourteen Crucial Episodes in American History* [1952], pp. 173–200), deals with the imperial impulse, re-emphasizing the idea that the acquisition of the Philippines was a turning point in American history. He rejects, for instance, the thesis that newspaper rivalry caused the Spanish-American War and seeks to find out why the American people were fatally receptive to war progapanda. He sees the answer in the light of social history and social psychology. In the "psychic economy of the nineties," he says, "war served as an outlet for aggressive impulses while presenting itself as an idealistic and humanitarian crusade. His interpretation thus states that

the war crisis and the acquisition of the Philippines are insep-
arable from "the psychic crisis of the 1890's."

In *The Imperial Years* (1956) Foster Rhea Dulles covers the
years of the new manifest destiny, basically from 1885 when Grover
Cleveland took office to 1909 when Theodore Roosevelt left the
White House. Also stressing the imperialist impulse, Dulles points
out that in these years the conflict between realism and idealism
in foreign policy "became greatly accentuated." He makes his
contribution in a readable synthesis that combines fact, ideas and
interpretation.

Centering his study on the ideas and action of one man, Howard
K. Beale in *Theodore Roosevelt and the Rise of America to
World Power* (1956) probed the ideological background of American imperialism and the motives of American statesmen. He also
tried to answer some of the large questions that have always puz-
zled historians. He asked, for example, what caused the United
States in the twentieth century to take the road it did in foreign
policy? Were the decisions of individual men responsible or were
blind forces decisive? His thesis stated that "a few men in powerful positions were able to plunge the nation into an imperialist
career that it never explicitly decided to follow." The taking of
the Philippines, he wrote, "was important history made not by
economic forces or democratic decisions but through the grasping
of chance authority by a man with daring and a program." This
book reflects the enlarged scope of American diplomatic history.
It uses ideas, and places American foreign policy in a setting of
world politics.

Two books trace a special development of the new manifest
destiny, expansion into Hawaii. In *American Expansion in Hawaii, 1842–1898* (1945) Sylvester K. Stevens' thesis states that "the
ultimate annexation of Hawaii in 1898 was the product of typical
American frontier expansion, and not a sporadic adventure in
imperialism occasioned by the circumstances connected with the
Spanish-Americain War." William A. Russ, Jr., in *The Hawaiian
Revolution, 1893–94* (1959), however, maintains that the American minister's actions in Hawaii during the revolution cannot be
justified morally or politically and stresses corruption in Queen

Liliuokalani's government as a basic cause for annexationist sentiment among American-Hawaiians.

THE FIRST WORLD WAR

As they have done with other wars, American historians in
studying the First World War have produced a polemical literature. Most of their controversial interpretations center on why
the United States intervened. Although the literature is large
and the interpretations vary in detail and scope, two schools of
thought are clear. One school analyzed the road to war and con-
cluded that the United States was justified and did right in going
to war. The other, the "revisionist" school, studied intervention
and said it was a mistake. Richard W. Leopold, in "The Problems of American Intervention, 1917: An Historical Retrospect"
(see *World Politics*, II [April, 1950], 404–425), has surveyed that
literature in detail, as has Ernest R. May in *American Intervention: 1917 and 1941* (1960).

After the Second World War broke out, two journalists, un-
doubtedly influenced by contemporary international politics,
stressed a new interpretation as to why the United States went to
war in 1917. Forrest Davis, in *The Atlantic System: The Story of
Anglo-American Control of the Seas* (1941) and Walter Lippmann,
in *U. S. Foreign Policy: Shield of the Republic* (1943), said the
United States intervened in 1917 to protect its own security. Ar-
min Rappaport, in *The British Press and Wilsonian Neutrality*
(1951), stresses the traditional interpretation that Germany's use
of the submarine drove the United States to war but also links
intervention to national interest. He concludes that "only when
the national interests of the United States were threatened by the
submarine did America go to war."

Samuel R. Spencer, in *Decision for War, 1917: The Laconia
Sinking and the Zimmermann Telegram as key Factors in the
Public Reaction Against Germany* (1953), shows how events of
February and March 1917 increased anti-German sentiment in
the United States. He rejects the revisionist arguments and de-
fends American entry into the war.

Thomas A. Bailey, in *Wilson and the Peacemakers* (1947), reflects a trend of assigning more responsibility to Wilson himself for failures in foreign policy than did earlier writers. For example, he rejects the conventional interpretation that Senator Henry Cabot Lodge and "bitter-end" senators were entirely responsible for the defeat of the Treaty of Versailles. He lays most of the blame for the failure on Wilson.

Arthur S. Link, in *Woodraw Wilson and the Progressive Era, 1910–1917* (1954), is also critical of Wilson's diplomacy, particularly of his "missionary diplomacy" in Mexico. As to war with Germany, he stresses the conventional interpretation that the submarine brought on the war but the final decision for war or peace came from Wilson himself. Link stresses the same conclusion, but in greater detail, in his small volume of lectures, *Wilson the Diplomatist* (1957). In his interpretation of Wilson as a diplomat, he suggests that given the alternatives open to Wilson because of Germany's submarine campaign, which Link considers overwhelmingly flagrant, the President had virtually no choice but that of war.

A similar thesis is advanced by Ernest R. May in *The World War and American Isolation* (1959). May says that the decision for war grew out of a contest within Wilson's conscience, that Wilson had staked American prestige on his diplomacy and that when German submarine warfare torpedoed his diplomacy he had to intervene to defend American prestige. May writes of Wilson's diplomacy that a "close analysis cannot find the point at which he might have turned back or taken another road."

A Swedish scholar, Karl E. Birnbaum, in *Peace Moves and U-Boat Warfare: A Study of Imperial Germany's Policy Towards the United States, April 18, 1916–January 9, 1917* (1958), uses hitherto unexploited German documents to place the submarine question and hence America's entry into the First World War against the background of German internal politics. In effect, this book, as does May's shows the importance of German public opinion and the military influence on the government in the events that led to American intervention. Birnbaum concludes that the foremost aim of German policy towards the United States was to keep it out of the war but that policy "pendulated between peace moves and submarine warfare."

Edward H. Buehrig, in *Woodrow Wilson and the Balance of Power* (1955), attempts to refute the generally accepted view that Wilson's idealism dominated foreign policy and hence conditioned American policy in the First World War. The United States intervened, he says, because it shrank from the prospect of Germany supplanting British power that contributed to American security. Concern over Germany's violation of American maritime rights, he concludes, was not therefore the reason for America's war against Germany. He stresses that Wilson had "an appreciation of the balance of power view." Beuhrig has also edited *Woodrow Wilson's Foreign Policy in Perspective* (1957), a small book of lectures by eminent scholars which, on the whole, tends to vindicate Wilson's foreign policy, even some of its idealism.

In *Robert Lansing and American Neutrality, 1914–1917* (1958), Daniel M. Smith stresses the familiar interpertations of why America went to war, but also advances the thesis that Lansing was more important in formulating and carrying out foreign policy than historians have generally conceded. Lansing, the author says, "bore a large share of the responsibility for American intervention in the war." Contrary to the views of other diplomatic historians, Louis A. R. Yates, in *United States and French Security, 1917–1921: A Study in American Diplomatic History* (1957), maintains that Wilson negotiated the guarantee treaties with France and Britain at Versailles in good faith and did not suspect that the treaties would inevitably die in the Senate.

THE HARDING-COOLIDGE-HOOVER ERA

Taking up some main strands of foreign policy after the Wilson years, Robert H. Ferrell has written two books on the diplomacy of the 1920's and 1930's. In *Peace in Their Time: The Origins of the Kellogg-Briand Pact* (1952), he praises American diplomats and is critical of public opinion. "Public ignorance," he believes, "created a serious problem in the conduct of American diplomacy" in the 1920's. Well-intentioned diplomats, he says, were handicapped because they "had to cope with a public opinion whose only virtue often was that it was public and opinionated."

In *American Diplomacy in the Great Depression: Hoover-Stimson Foreign Policy, 1929–1933* (1957), Ferrell has widened the scope of his history, presenting the thesis that American diplomacy in the Hoover era in effect failed in its grand purpose, the preservation of peace. The overriding reason for the failure, he says, was the great depression which "palsied the hands of American statesmen." Other reasons were, he explains, a legalistic approach to diplomacy and a false reliance on a policy of moral suasion predicated on the mistaken assumption of a continuing international equilibrium. Lastly, he maintains that the problems flowing from the events themselves were so baffling as virtually to defy mastery by American statesmen, competent though they were.

Paralleling Ferrell's studies, J. Chalmers Vinson, in *The Parchment Peace: The United States Senate and the Washington Conference, 1921–1922* (1955), reflects one of the new approaches to the study of American foreign policy by analyzing the role of the Senate in shaping foreign policy. His interpretation is critical of that role. He points out that the Senate hailed the Washington treaties as a contribution to peace. Yet, in approving them, it would not allow the United States to assume obligations for maintaining peace. It, like the American people, had faith in a "new diplomacy of trust."

THE SECOND WORLD WAR

Like the First World War the second generated a large controversial literature on the causes of America's participation and on the motives of the statesmen who led the nation into the war. Soon after, the war memoirs of many of the major statesmen, biographies, and studies of the foreign policy of the period, appeared. Those books, while differing in detail, emphasis, and in interpretation, showed a sharp division on the causes of America's going to war and on the motives of American statesmen.

On one side were those who either defended the foreign policy of President Franklin D. Roosevelt or supported the thesis that the United States had gone to war to protect its own security. They argued that Roosevelt had no desire to lead the country to war. While admitting some deviousness on Roosevelt's part, they excused it because they felt that short-sighted isolationist opposition to his policies blocked forthright measures essential to protect the nation's security. They advanced what most historians would call the "conventional" interpretation of the foreign policy of the period.

On the other side were those who challenged the conventional assumptions and attacked Roosevelt's foreign policy. They charged the President and his advisers with leading the country to war while professing to work for peace. Their theory says that the nation went to war unnecessarily. Some of them argue that in fighting fascism the United States overlooked a greater menace, communism. These writers and historians comprise the new "revisionist" school of diplomatic historians. For a detailed discussion of the literature of both schools see Wayne S. Cole, "American Entry into World War II: A Historiographical Appraisal" (see *The Mississippi Valley Historical Review*, XLIII [March, 1957], 597–617).

In an effort to allay the bitterness of the new revisionist agitation, the Council on Foreign Relations sponsored a detailed study of American foreign policy in the crisis leading to war. This project resulted in the two detailed books by William L. Langer and S. Everett Gleason, *The Challenge to Isolation, 1937–1940* (1952), and *The Undeclared War, 1940–1941* (1953). The authors deny that Roosevelt plotted to involve the country in war. They hold that he actually lagged behind public opinion in moving toward intervention, and that he formulated his foreign policy to avoid war.

The Langer volumes did not succeed in allaying the revisionist bitterness. Instead, they appeared to increase it. Revisionists said that Langer and Gleason, because of previous official connections with the government and because they offered little that criticized government officials, were merely "court historians" and that they had written a "whitewash" of Roosevelt's foreign policy.

Two books that do not belong strictly in the revisionist school but are highly critical of Roosevelt's wartime diplomacy are Hanson W. Baldwin's *Great Mistakes of the War* (1950) and Richard N. Current's *Secretary Stimson: A Study in Statecraft* (1954). Baldwin's thesis holds that Roosevelt's foreign and war policies and decisions made postwar problems more difficult than they would have been anyway. He calls the policy of unconditional surrender "the biggest political mistake of the war." Current attacks Secretary Henry L. Stimson's ideas and actions in foreign policy. His thesis declares that "a whole blundering generation of American statesmen" led the nation into a war that might have been avoided.

By placing most of the blame for war with Japan on the United States, Paul W. Schroeder, in *The Axis Alliance and Japanese-American Relations, 1941* (1958), also follows a revisionist theme. The "real cause of the war," he argues, was America's uncompromising stand on China. That policy of making China's integrity paramount was wrong. If the United States had followed a more conciliatory policy, there could have been an alternative to war. He also advances the interpretation that the Axis alliance posed no real threat to the United States and was not an important factor in the outbreak of war with Japan.

Hans L. Trefousse, in *Germany and American Neutrality, 1939–1941* (1951), on the other hand shows that Adolf Hitler finally declared war on the United States because, in part at least, of his obligation to Japan. Trefousse, in addition, advances the view that German leaders exercised conspicuous restraint toward the United States because they sought to avoid bringing another major power into the war against them. He also maintains that Hitler underestimated American war potential.

While tracing the planning for the occupation and fate of defeated Nazi Germany, John L. Snell, in *Wartime Origins of the East-West Dilemma over Germany* (1959), says that American policy in that planning was haphazard, one of postponement. Snell also edited a book of essays, *The Meaning of Yalta: Big Three Diplomacy and the New Balance of Power* (1956), that presents the thesis that the United States did not give away anything at Yalta that was within its power to withhold, hence there was no betrayal there. In explaining the meaning of Yalta, the authors say that "personal diplomacy at Yalta came to grips with the basic realities of a new balance of power in the world at large, and the freedom of the individual statesmen was greatly restricted by these impersonal forces."

Herbert Feis has written the two most important books on American foreign policy during the Second World War. The first, *Churchill, Roosevelt, Stalin: The War They Waged and the*

Peace They Sought (1957), carried the record of Allied diplomacy through the Yalta Conference of February 1945. Unlike critics of Franklin D. Roosevelt, such as Hanson Baldwin, Feis maintains that the doctrine of unconditional surrender did not mean anni- hilation or merciless punishment for the Germans or Japanese and interprets the doctrine as having little effect on the conduct or outcome of the war. The second book, *Between War and Peace: The Potsdam Conference* (1960), continues the chronicle through the Potsdam Conference in July 1945. Feis believes that mutual confidence between the wartime allies ended at Potsdam and that the Grand Alliance began to fall apart there. By analyz- ing that breakup, he exposes the roots of the cold war and advances the thesis that the three great allies, the United States, the Soviet Union and Great Britain, needed to maintain trust and friendship between themselves for a stable postwar world and failed. This, he maintains, was the tragedy of Allied diplomacy.

Paul Kecskemeti, in *Strategic Surrender: The Politics of Victory and Defeat* (1958), analyzes the concept of strategic surrender not as a question of military strategy but as a problem in political the- ory. He agrees with Feis that the doctrine of unconditional sur- render did not prolong the war.

Sixteen experts in East European history wrote essays, in Stephen D. Kertesz, ed., *The Fate of East Central Europe: Hopes and Failures of American Foreign Policy* (1956), tracing American relations with the countries of East Central Europe. One theme appears to permeate the volume, that there cannot be effective diplomacy without adequate military power. Because there were no American troops there, they point out, East Central Europe fell to the mercy of the Soviet Union. Edward J. Rozek, in *Allied Wartime Diplomacy: A Pattern in Poland* (1958), deals with one country in that part of Europe. He attempts to refute the thesis that Russia's failure to live up to the Yalta Agreement placed Poland behind the iron curtain. He maintains, in effect, that American and British agreements with the Soviet Union, though not deliberately, betrayed Poland. "The enslavement of Poland," he concludes, "was the price the Western Powers had to pay for their belief that Soviet verbal promises could be trusted."

In *A History of the United Nations Charter: The Role of the*

United States, 1940–1945 (1958) Ruth B. Russell has written a basic reference work on the important issues the United States faced in the drafting of the charter. She stresses the development of the charter as a part of American foreign policy and shows that when the charter entered into force in October 1945 "the international co-operation necessary to fulfill the United Nations system was already undermined."

THE TRUMAN-EISENHOWER YEARS

Although James P. Warburg, in *The United States in a Changing World: An Historical Analysis of American Foreign Policy* (1954), covers the whole of American diplomatic history his unique contribution is his interpretive and critical synthesis of the international crisis after the Second World War, which he explains as stemming from two outstanding developments. He sees the first as the change in the distribution of power in the Western world from Western Europe to the United States and in the nature of that power through the invention of atomic weapons of mass destruction. The second development, he maintains, is a worldwide revolution, which did not grow primarily from a communist conspiracy but from the material progress of Western civilization that has aroused the underprivilegd two-thirds of mankind. Truman and his advisers, Warburg argues, did not face these facts but instead adopted a "devil-theory of world crisis" that placed all the blame on the Soviet Union. By committing themselves to the negative policy of containment, he concludes, Truman's policymakers missed an opportunity to lead the revolutionary forces in the world and perhaps resolve the crisis.

H. Bradford Westerfield, in *Foreign Policy and Party Politics: Pearl Harbor to Korea* (1955), has studied Congress' treatment of issues in foreign policy on the basis of "partisanship" and "bipartisanship" and its influence in the making of policy. He argues that there is greater need for a broad consensus, for predictability and continuity, in foreign policy than in domestic policy, and that these can be achieved only through some measure of collaboration between the major political parties.

The Fifteen Weeks, February 21–June 5, 1947 (1955), by Joseph M. Jones, a participant in the policymaking described, tells the story of the launching of the Truman Doctrine and the Marshall Plan. He offers the thesis that those two events were key developments signaling a transformation of American foreign policy that led to far-reaching results, actually to the policy of containment and the diplomatic battles of the cold war. The first survey of the Marshall Plan as a whole is offered by Harry B. Price, in *The Marshall Plan and Its Meaning* (1955), who points out that though it was not directed against any country, "it was nevertheless a defense against the Soviet threat."

The theoretical foundations of the policy of containment were advanced by George F. Kennan, writing as Mr. "X", in "The Sources of Soviet Conduct" (see *Foreign Affairs*, XXV [July 1947], 556–582). He argued that "the Soviet pressure against the free institutions of the Western world is something that can be contained by the adroit and vigilant application of counter-force at a series of constantly shifting geographical and political points corresponding to the shifts and maneuvers of Soviet policy . . ."

The concept of the bipartisan foreign policy receives close analysis in Cecil V. Crabb, *Bipartisan Foreign Policy: Myth or Reality?* (1957). Crabb maintains that the bipartisan approach has neither met the expectations of dedicated adherents nor justified the cries of severe critics. While conceding virtues to such an approach, he concludes that they are outweighed by its faults.

John W. Spanier, in *The Truman-MacArthur Controversy and the Korean War* (1959), seeks to find whether the principle of civilian supremacy over the military is compatible with the waging of limited war. He answers that if war is a political tool as maintained by Karl von Clausewitz, the German theorist, then military operations must be subordinate to political aims and that military operations cannot be conducted in an autonomous sphere unencumbered by "outside interference." No government, he maintains, can allow a military officer to challenge publicly its whole foreign policy without undermining its authority to determine the nation's policy, dividing the public support it needs and alienating the allies it desires.

In *The United States in the World Arena: An Essay in Recent History* (1960) Walt W. Rostow advances a novel interpretation. In surveying two decades of American foreign policy, from the beginning of the Second World War to 1958, he tries to show how the "national style," i.e. how the United States has typically attempted to solve its problems, has affected its performance in foreign policy. He contends that the national style is in a process of change and that it must change to protect the national interest in a world where power is being rapidly diffused.

John C. Campbell, in *Defense of the Middle East: Problems of American Policy* (1958, rev. ed., 1960), presents a brief account of the development of American policy in the Middle East and tries to analyze the problems confronting policymakers who are concerned with the defense of that region against Soviet encroachment.

New techniques for the study of foreign policy are used in Karl W. Deutsch and others, *Political Community and the North Atlantic Area: International Organization in the Light of Historical Experience* (1957). On the basis of historical observation, the authors have tried to ascertain if a community of states can prevent war from breaking out among its members. Most of the data comes from price movements and demographic evolution in the countries studied. As long as the North Atlantic Alliance remains in force, the authors suggest, the danger of war among the member states is remote, but that alliance will disappear when danger from communism diminishes and then the possibility of war among the North Atlantic states will reappear.

FAR EASTERN RELATIONS

A. Whitney Griswold, in *The Far Eastern Policy of the United States* (1938), interprets American policy in Asia as having antagonized other powers without having achieved anything for the United States. After examining the open door policy, he concludes that Secretary of State John Hay had not secured international support for the open door principles, but "had merely oriented American policy toward a more active participation in Far Eastern politics in support of those principles."

In *God, Mammon, and the Japanese: Dr. Horace N. Allen and Korean-American Relations, 1884–1905* (1944) Fred H. Harrington weaves religious and economic factors into a diplomatic study.

He analyzes the commercial and diplomatic side of missionary work in the Far East. Charles S. Campbell, Jr., in *Special Business Interests and the Open Door Policy* (1951), has studied the role of American business interests in foreign policy in the Far East and points out that those interests played a decisive part in bringing about Hay's open door policy.

Paul A. Varg, in *Open Door Diplomat: The Life of W. W. Rockhill* (1952), has also examined the open door policy and writes that it was not Alfred E. Hippisley but William W. Rockhill who attempted to connect that policy with the preservation of the Chinese empire. Varg attempts to revise the earlier interpretation that the open door notes were concerned solely with equality of commercial opportunity, saying that Rockhill wanted to preserve China's integrity and independence as a necessary condition to an open door.

In *Missionaries, Chinese, and Diplomats; The American Protestant Missionary Movement in China, 1890–1952* (1958) Varg analyzed the role of the missionaries in American Far Eastern policy and the reasons for their failure. He maintains that the missionary effort, as a phase of the American impact on China, was so alien to Chinese culture that early in the 1950's Chinese Marxism and nationalism snuffed it out. He attributes little direct influence to the missionaries as a pressure group in the shaping of American foreign policy, but says they did help, in a larger context, to shape America's image of China.

William R. Braisted's *The United States Navy in the Pacific, 1897–1909* (1958), a study of the Navy's influence on foreign policy, points out that America's naval policies of trying to obtain a naval base on the coast of China and to establish one in the Philippines failed because of Japan's victory in her war with Russia. He concludes that the role of the Navy in the Pacific as the strong right arm of diplomacy, even though important, was unimpressive.

Raymond A. Esthus, in "The Taft-Katsura Agreement—Reality or Myth?" (see *The Journal of Modern History*, XXXI [March, 1959], 46–51), rejects the old interpretation that the Taft-Katsura "agreed memorandum" of 1905 was a secret bargain in which Japan renounced designs on the Philippine Islands in return for American acquiescence in its control of Korea. He shows there was no "secret pact" or "agreement" and suggests that the Taft-Katsura conversation represented nothing more than "an honest exchange of views."

In *The United States and China, 1906–1913: A Study of Finance and Diplomacy* (1955), Charles Vevier has concentrated on economics in foreign policy, especially on the thinking and ambitions of the American financiers and diplomats who took an active part in shaping the policy of dollar diplomacy in China and Manchuria. Like Griswold, he is critical of President William H. Taft's China policy and of his shopkeeper or dollar diplomacy.

Three books that deal with related parts of President Woodrow Wilson's policy in the Far East are *Woodrow Wilson and the Far East: The Diplomacy of the Shantung Question* (1952) by Russell H. Fifield; *Woodrow Wilson's China Policy, 1913–1917* (1952) by Tien-yi Li; and *Woodrow Wilson and Far Eastern Policy, 1913–1921* (1957) by Roy W. Curry. Fifield devotes most of his attention to the Shantung question, particularly to its diplomacy at the Paris Peace Conference in 1919. Through the Shantung question he explains other diplomatic problems because he considers it "within the frame of reference of world politics." He treats Wilson's diplomacy favorably, saying Wilson "retreated from his position in the Shantung controvery because he wanted to insure Japanese membership in the League of Nations." This study is an example of how the student of international relations has also become a student of American foreign policy.

Tien-yi Li is critical of Wilson's policy in China up to 1917. He says Wilson's "policy of maintaining China's integrity was largely a failure." In the long run China suffered from that policy, he believes, because the President followed ethical rather than practical considerations. Covering a broader period, Curry treats Wilson more favorably. He says Wilson, who "initiated little in the way of Far Eastern policy," followed methods that fitted traditional American policy in the Far East. "There was never any master strategy," Curry concludes, "beyond support for the historic policies pursued in relation to the area."

Betty M. Unterberger, in *America's Siberian Expedition, 1918–1920: A Study of National Policy* (1956), explains that Wilson's "basic and unpublicized" reason for intervention in Siberia "was to restrain Japan from imperialistic adventures and to preserve the open door in Siberia and North Manchuria." The United States, she believes, prevented Japan from going into Russia alone and with a free hand. "The positive results of the intervention," she concludes, "were due largely to American participation."

In a study of later Far Eastern policy, *The China Tangle: The American Effort in China from Pearl Harbor to the Marshall Mission* (1953), Herbert Feis also criticizes American policy. In dealing with the American effort to bring China into a more effective role in the Second World War, he feels that American officials misjudged the Chinese Communists. His thesis suggests that the spirit of the times, ignorance of the Communists, Russian diplomacy, distrust of Chinese Nationalists, and blunders, produced the failure of American foreign policy in China.

In *Japanese and Americans: A Century of Cultural Relations* (1955), Robert S. Schwantes stressed international cultural relations, specifically between Japan and the United States in the areas of economic co-operation, political institutions and ideology, and education. He suggests that when economic and political issues are dealt with properly, sympathetic cultural contacts become substantially important and may even transcend collective national interest.

Bernard C. Cohen, in *The Political Process and Foreign Policy: The Making of the Japanese Peace Settlement* (1957), using the method of case analysis, explored the negotiations leading to the peace settlement with Japan as a means of developing a theory on the making of foreign policy or at least a method for the systematic study of the process of forming foreign policy. He offers a number of hypotheses on the making of foreign policy and maintains that the success of the treaty settlement stemmed from the skill of John Foster Dulles. In another case study, *Korea: A Study of United States Policy in the United Nations* (1956), Leland M. Goodrich emphasized the interrelation of the Korean policies of the United States and of the United Nations. His thesis is that after the outbreak of the Korean War, the United States in cooperation with other members of the United Nations showed that "aggression" did not pay and also succeeded in keeping the Korean War from spreading into a worldwide conflict.

The essays in George L. Anderson (ed.), *Issues and Conflicts: Studies in Twentieth Century American Diplomacy* (1959) contain interpretive analyses in a wide range of subjects. William L. Neumann's essay, "Determinism, Destiny, and Myth in the American Image of China," pp. 1–22, reflects a recent trend in the direction of seeing ideas as images and certain concepts as myths. National images, he says, are composed more of myth than reality, "while 'national security' appears as the fantasy of exuberant patriots." Maintaining that students of international relations have neglected the role of myth and irrationality in the making of foreign policy because of the difficulties of assessing collective behavior, he sketches the myth in the concept of American destiny in China. That myth, he suggests, concealed from Americans such realities as the intensity of the antiforeignism of Chinese nationalism and the appeals of communism to the Chinese.

In *The China Lobby in American Politics* (1960) Ross Y. Koen examines the techniques of intervention of the "China lobby" in American politics and its influence on Far Eastern policy. He concludes that such a lobby functioned from the beginning of the Second World War on and was staffed by paid agents of Chiang Kai-shek. "The most significant point about the entire development," he says, "is that the China lobby view of events was widely accepted" and tragically influenced the conduct of American foreign policy.

LATIN AMERICAN POLICY

Recent literature on relations with Latin America has tended to be critical of our policy in that part of the world and much of it has emphasized various aspects of the good neighbor policy. Samuel F. Bemis' *The Latin American Policy of the United States: An Historical Interpretation* (1943) offers an exception to the trend of critical interpretations. His nationalistic defense of our Latin American policy challenges accepted ideas as to the merits of that policy. According to his thesis, that policy was determined primarily by considerations of the "Continental Republic," first in North America and then in the western hemisphere as a whole.

In one of the first books to deal with the question of origin,

Alexander DeConde's *Herbert Hoover's Latin American Policy* (1951) suggests that the good neighbor policy began in the Hoover administration. His interpretation points out that Franklin D. Roosevelt later adopted, expanded and made that policy his own.

Concentrating on the period Roosevelt held office, Edward O. Guerrant, in *Roosevelt's Good Neighbor Policy* (1950), maintains that "the United States has never had a foreign policy toward any area that was more successful than the Good Neighbor Policy was from 1933 to 1945." Edmund D. Cronon's *Josephus Daniels in Mexico* (1960) advances the view that Mexico in the 1930's gave the good neighbor policy its severest test, yet throughout the difficulties Ambassador Daniels remained the champion of a true neighborly approach. The settlement with Mexico in 1941, dealing with expropriated American oil companies in Mexico, Cronon says, climaxed Daniels' patient labors and touched the high-water mark of good neighbor diplomacy.

Donald M. Dozer, in *Are We Good Neighbors? Three Decades of Inter-American Relations, 1930–1960* (1959), maintains that "the normal state of Latin America is to be hostile to the United States" and that the hostility persists. He points out that the good neighbor policy paid off during the depression and in the Second World War. Like Guerrant and others, he says that after 1945 relations with Latin America deteriorated.

Edwin Lieuwen, in *Arms and Politics in Latin America* (1960), attempts to analyze one reason for the deterioration by studying the armed forces in Latin America and their influence on the interests and policies of the United States. He suggests that the concern for military security in United States policy toward Latin America in the 1950's is not in keeping with the long-range interests of the United States and threatens to ruin the nation's entire Latin American policy. To create a more favorable image among Latin Americans, he says, the United States should aid democratic governments not dictatorships and should reduce its emphasis on military considerations.

Two other books deal with a form of Pan Americanism, or what one historian calls the western hemisphere idea. "The core of the Western Hemisphere idea," Arthur P. Whitaker wrote in his book *The Western Hemisphere Idea: Its Rise and Decline* (1954), "has been the proposition that the peoples of this Hemisphere stand in a special relationship to one another which sets them apart from the rest of the world." In what is essentially a study of diplomatic and intellectual history, Whitaker stresses the crucial part the United States played in the development and application of that idea, which always found its best expression in politics and diplomacy. He states that the idea came closest to becoming fact during the Second World War, but lost its hold on the minds of Americans to the north and declined in the postwar years. It has, Whitaker says, been kept alive mainly by Latin Americans.

J. Fred Rippy, in *Globe and Hemisphere: Latin America's Place in the Postwar Foreign Relations of the United States* (1958), also stresses the western hemisphere concept, maintaining that the unique community that idea helped to shape still exists and should serve as the "inner fortress" for the United States in its commitment to power politics on a worldwide scale. He suggests, for instance, that "if the Western Hemisphere can be developed into a model of harmony, prosperity, democracy, and liberty, let this be done for the benefit of the Hemisphere and the rest of the globe."

RELATIONS WITH RUSSIA

Much of the new literature on relations with Russia that flows from the presses in vast quantities is of limited scholarly value when dealing with the Soviet era because of Soviet censorship and refusal to allow scholars access to documents. Like the warp of a garment, moreover, the theme of Soviet-American rivalry runs through most of it and through almost any book on American foreign policy written since 1947.

Thomas A. Bailey, in *America Faces Russia: Russian-American Relations from Early Times to Our Day* (1950), shows that the United States and Russia did not share a long unbroken friendship running from the beginning of American independence through the nineteenth century. According to his interpretation, the basis of whatever friendship existed was mutual hostility to England.

In *American-Russian Relations, 1781–1947* (1952), William A.

Williams interprets America's difficulties with Russia in a different light. He views them as stemming from hostile and even aggressive policies toward Russia.

In a study published the following year, *The Origins of Soviet-American Diplomacy*, Robert P. Browder concentrated on the negotiations leading up to American recognition of the Soviet Union in 1933. He believes that in agreeing to recognition the United States covered up underlying disagreements and differences in concepts and aims between the Soviets and itself and hence left basic issues unresolved.

George F. Kennan, in *Soviet-American Relations, 1917–1920*, Vol. I, *Russia Leaves the War* (1956), differs with those "who were inclined to assign exclusively to the United States government the blame for an unhappy state of relations between the two governments." He stresses the hatred of Soviet leaders for Western capitalism and denies that the United States rejected the friendship they offered and "thus needlessly estranged them in the early days of their power, when they desperately needed sympathy and support." One goal in the Soviet leaders' flirting with the United States, he points out, was to forestall Japanese intervention in Siberia.

In his second volume, *The Decision to Intervene* (1958), Kennan advances the interpretation that Wilson decided to intervene in northern Russia under French and British pressure and chose to do so in Siberia to aid Czechoslovakian troops stranded there. In effect, he rejects the view that the United States sent troops to smother communism in its cradle. That double intervention, in which Wilson overruled his military advisers, Kennan maintains, was ill-advised and marks the beginning of a long tragedy. He concludes that "the reasons for this failure of American statesmanship lay . . . in such things as the deficiencies of the American political system from the standpoint of the conduct of foreign relations . . . and the pervasive dilettantism in the execution of American policy."

ISOLATIONISM

Historians and others have shown a continuing interest in isolationism. Many of the books discussed in this pamphlet include sections dealing with it, but until the past few years the historians have not focused their full attention on isolationism itself. Much of the literature on the subject, therefore, as the following noteworthy studies show, has been made up of tentative broad interpretations and has lacked investigation in depth among the sources.

J. Fred Rippy, in *America and the Strife of Europe* (1938), outlines relations with Europe boldly and subjects American foreign policy, particularly isolation, to critical analysis. He deals with broad subjects: isolation, the pacifist movement, expansion, and others. Along with other scholars, he believes that the strife and troubles of Europe largely made possible isolation and the success of American foreign policy since independence. While his thesis was not new, his broad interpretation of ideas and movements in American foreign policy was unique for its time.

Two books, Walter Johnson's *The Battle Against Isolation* (1944) and Wayne S. Cole's *America First: The Battle Against Intervention, 1940–1941* (1953), offer specialized appraisals of isolationism just prior to America's entry into the Second World War in the stories of the two major groups that sought to represent and influence public opinion. Johnson deals with The Committee to Defend America by Aiding the Allies, the most prominent organization that fought isolationism, and Cole analyzes the methods and techniques of the America First Committee, the most powerful mass pressure isolationist, or noninterventionist, group in the country. Both studies stress the great part public opinion, particularly as generated by private organizations, played in influencing foreign policy before the attack on Pearl Harbor.

Finally, in 1957, Selig Adler brought together the various strands of ideas that made up modern isolationism and wrote the first book-length history from the sources in *The Isolationist Impulse: Its Twentieth Century Reaction*. Writing from the viewpoint of an "internationalist" and concentrating on the years from 1914 to 1956, he dissects the various propaganda and pressure groups that attempted to shape mass opinion and made isolationism prominent. In his treatment of the impact of ideas on foreign policy he thus combines conventional diplomatic history with intellectual history.

A similar but brief treatment can be found in *Isolation and Security: Ideas and Interests in Twentieth-Century American Foreign Policy* (1957), edited by Alexander DeConde. In this collection of seven interpretive essays by different authors, isolationism is presented as part of the theme of American foreign policy between the two world wars, a theme of isolationism *versus* collective security. The conclusion states that both ideas failed to provide a sound theoretical foundation for foreign policy.

Ray Allen Billington, in "The Origins of Middle Western Isolationism" (see *Political Science Quarterly*, LX [March, 1945], 44–64), advances a provocative sectional and ethnic interpretation of isolationism in the twentieth century. He suggests that isolationist sentiment in the Midwest stemmed largely from the inherited customs and prejudices of German and Scandinavian immigrants and their offspring. Their "prejudices and attitudes, bolstered by the sense of security which grew from the section's geographic position and economic self-sufficiency," he writes, "help to explain Middle Western isolationism."

In *The New Isolationism: A Study in Politics and Foreign Policy Since 1950* (1956), Norman A. Graebner concentrates on the effects on American diplomacy of certain internal political forces. He believes that the new isolationists of the 1950's were "the true heirs" of the old isolationist tradition. His thesis is that the new isolationism "reflected the deepest traditions of suspicion, distrust, and withdrawal from the world, as well as the deep conviction that an isolated America could live securely without allies, overseas commitments, or military preparedness even at mid-century."

Another regional study of isolationism, Alexander DeConde's "The South and Isolationism" (see *The Journal of Southern History*, XXIV [August, 1958], 332–346), analyzes the South's new, or postwar, isolationism and suggests that southern "internationalism" was no stronger that that of other regions, except under special circumstances as in the Second World War. Paul Seabury, in a pamphlet, *The Waning of Southern "Internationalism"* (1957), touches a similar theme.

In *The United States and the Spanish Civil War* (1956), Foster Jay Taylor examines the nature of American opinion during that conflict and the political factors which influenced Franklin D. Roosevelt's administration in formulating its policy toward the Spanish regimes. He states that the desire to avoid involvement in war, expressed as isolationism in America opinion, exerted the strongest pressure on Roosevelt and the government. Religious and ideological factors, mainly those of Catholicism and anti-Catholicism, fascism and communism, bred controversy and blurred the focus of public opinion.

Bernard Fensterwald, Jr., in "The Anatomy of American Isolationism and Expansionism" (see *The Journal of Conflict Resolution*, II [June and December, 1958], 111–139, 280–309), attempts to use various kinds of data, especially sociological and psychological materials, to explain isolationism. He tries to demonstrate that isolationism and expansionism are closely related expressions of nationalism and have compatible psychological bases. His thesis maintains that attitudes favoring isolationism, or aloofness from Europe, and expansionism in other parts of the world can be explained on the basis of psychological compatibility as well as historical evidence.

MILITARY STRATEGY AND FOREIGN POLICY

Since the Second World War various writers, but political scientists more than historians, have stressed the close relationship between military strategy and diplomacy, armaments and foreign policy. A steady stream of new books on this subject attests to its importance and perhaps to a newly won popularity, even among scholars. A pioneer study in this area was Harold and Margaret Sprout's, *The Rise of American Naval Power* (1939) and one of the first to deal with "armament or disarmament policy" was Merze Tate whose book, *The United States and Armaments* (1948), is a history of the part played by the American government in the movement for the limitation of armaments. "Disarmament," Tate maintains, "is not a moral, not a mathematical, not a technical, but a political problem; while armaments are merely the means by which states seek to give effect to their national policies."

Walter Millis, in *Arms and Men: A Study in American Military*

History (1956), expounds the idea that in the nuclear age total war will bring universal catastrophe and hence cannot serve as the instrument of foreign policy as it has in the past. It is no longer available as the tool of foreign policy. If nations and peoples are to survive, therefore, they must resolve their differences by other means.

One of the most discussed books in recent years, Henry A. Kissinger's *Nuclear Weapons and Foreign Policy* (1957), fuses political and military ideas to offer a doctrine of limited war with nuclear weapons. The author presents foreign and military policy, peace and war, as different parts of an organic whole, the defense and promotion of the national interest in relations with other nations. He suggests that "foreign policy henceforth will have to be framed against the background of a world in which the 'conventional' technology is nuclear technology."

In *Arms and the State: Civil-Military Elements in National Politics* (1958) Walter Millis, Harvey C. Mansfield and Harold Stein also probe the theme of relations between the soldier and the civilian leader, mainly from 1933 to 1945, in American society. They maintain that lines can no longer be drawn clearly between military and political considerations in the making of national policy.

An economist and mathematician, Oskar Morgenstern, in *The Question of National Defense* (1959), laments that our diplomats are not trained in mathematics and technology and maintains that mathematicians can reconstruct war as an abstract reality. War, he says, can be reduced to a manageable enterprise through the use of mathematical tools, mainly through the use of sophisticated procedures as in "the domain of the mathematical theory of games of strategy, which has clarified the conceptual problem of decision making. . ."

In U. S. Department of the Army, Office of Military History, *Command Decisions* (1959), ed. Kent R. Greenfield, sixteen historians devote twenty essays to high-level decisions that materially affected military events from 1940 to 1945. A common theme appears to be that total war invites major strategic decisions by civilian leaders because those decisions involve politics and foreign policy.

IDEAS AND BROAD INTERPRETATIONS

A number of the works discussed under other headings concerned themselves with the ideological side of foreign policy, a concern that in the past few years has become virtually a trend. The following studies reflect that trend either in their emphasis on ideas and theory or in their efforts to advance interpretations on some broad areas of foreign policy.

Four French academicians, in André Allix and others, *Les fondements de la politique extérieure des États-Unis* (1949), tried to explain the basis of American foreign policy to their own people because of American dominance of international affairs and in so doing dealt mainly with ideas. The second essay, which considers the formation of American attitudes toward isolationism (idealism, realism and other matters in foreign affairs, suggests that American foreign policy can be understood in the light of a perhaps unique control exercised by public opinion. The thesis in the third essay maintains that only through interest in the Pacific, considered an extension of the American frontier, and its occupation in the final phase of the westward movement did a national foreign policy evolve.

Thomas A. Bailey, in *The Man in the Street: The Impact of American Public Opinion on Foreign Policy* (1949), takes a broad view of public opinion with a pioneer work that analyzes the influence of that opinion on foreign policy. According to his interpretation, public opinion is the most powerful force in American foreign policy, but is also ignorant and fickle.

In 1951 two books appeared that touched off an academic debate on whether American foreign policy should be moralistic or realistic. George F. Kennan's interpretation, in *American Diplomacy, 1900–1950*, in his own words, is this: "I see the most serious fault of our past policy formulation to lie in something that I might call the legalistic-moralistic approach to international problems. This approach runs like a red skein through our foreign policy of the last fifty years." Hans J. Morgenthau's *In Defense of the National Interest: A Critical Examination of American Foreign Policy* (1951) advances a similar thesis. He says that American foreign policy since the days of the Founding Fathers has been too moralistic and utopian. Only in the period following the Second World War, he believes, have Americans become realistic and again measured their foreign policies by the yardstick of power and "the national interest."

Thomas I. Cook and Malcolm Moos, in *Power Through Purpose: The Realism of Idealism as a Basis for Foreign Policy* (1954), take exception to the views of Kennan and Morgenthau. They urge that American foreign policy be based on ethical principles of "universal validity." They are opposed to "the extremes of utopian worldism and realistic nationalism."

Frank Tannenbaum, in *The American Tradition in Foreign Policy* (1955), also refutes the Kennan-Morgenthau thesis, attacking those who would adopt the doctrine of the balance of power as the basis of American foreign policy. He says that doctrine "runs counter to the very essence of the American tradition." He argues that belief in ideals has always been the American philosophy of international relations.

Another book that deals with realism, idealism, and power politics is *Ideals and Self-Interest in America's Foreign Relations: The Great Transformation of the Twentieth Century* (1953), by Robert E. Osgood. The author's thesis is that ideals and self-interest are interdependent and that they should strike a balance in international relations. Since he stresses ideas and the ideological background of foreign policy, he too brings something of a fresh approach to the study of American diplomatic history.

Expressing a similar concern for the influence of ideas or concepts on foreign policy, Edward McNall Burns, in *The American Idea of Mission: Concepts of National Purpose and Destiny* (1957), has analyzed the idea of mission in American history, which he sees as a main clue to understanding the United States. Americans, he shows, had the notion that they possessed a peculiar God-given mission to carry the gospel of "freedom" and "equality" to the ends of the earth and must use military might, if necessary, to carry out that mission.

Louis J. Halle has placed foreign policy in a broad setting of ideas, major historical movements, the forms of society and civilization, and man's inner nature. To him foreign policy signifies "broad and general principles of conduct." Those principles, however, often do not work because of the conflict between the myths that govern a country's thinking and the realities of the world at given times. More often than not, he says in *Dream and Reality: Aspects of American Foreign Policy* (1959), foreign policy is built on myth. He maintains that the United States understood reality until the end of the nineteenth century, but then, when it took the Philippines, it got caught in the quicksand of Far Eastern politics and myth.

Following a similar theme, Doris A. Graber, in *Crisis Diplomacy: A History of U. S. Intervention Policies and Practices* (1959), a study that tries to disentangle the theory and practice of nonintervention, maintains that in the ninteenth century American leaders upheld a studied balance between national power and the specific interests to be guaranteed. They avoided objectives that might have exceeded the national interest or committed American power unwisely. At the turn of the century the change began. Then, intervention became accepted policy in Latin America and the Far East where opposing power was weak. Later, especially during the cold war, the United States advanced policies to influence events in Europe and elsewhere in the world.

While also stressing the twentieth century as the turning point in American diplomatic history, William A. Williams, in *The Tragedy of American Diplomacy* (1959), offers a broad economic interpretation of that history. He maintains that since the turn of the century American foreign policy has been governed by "open door imperialism," a program of economic expansion dictated by the nation's corporate leaders. That policy grew out of John Hay's open door notes on China but was broadened in later years with worldwide implications. The tragedy of "open door imperialism," he says, is its result. It has bred dislike and distrust of the United States throughout the world and caused the cold war.

Kenneth W. Thompson has written two books dealing with the ideas of realism and idealism. In the first, *Christian Ethics and the Dilemmas of Foreign Policy* (1959), he takes the position of a "Christian realist" as opposed to both political idealism and political realism. He denies that there are Christian principles of foreign policy in the sense that Christianity can supply rules of conduct for the makers of foreign policy. The Christian concepts of turning the other cheek or of repaying evil with good, he says, are meant to apply to individuals, not to nations. In *Political Realism and the Crisis of World Politics: An American Approach to Foreign Policy* (1960), he reviews ideas that have influenced American foreign policy in recent years, mainly political realism, by analyzing the works of other students of the subject. His interpretation suggests that a realistic or pragmatic approach to the world crisis he discussess, an approach that stresses the techniques and methods of diplomacy, offers intellectual resources sufficient for the conduct of foreign policy.

Dexter Perkins is probably the only American diplomatic historian in recent years who has advanced a theory covering the whole history of American foreign policy. In *The American Approach to Foreign Policy* (1952) he suggests that there is a rhythm to the history of American foreign policy which *"may* have a connection with the movements of the business cycle." He calls this "A Cyclical Theory of American Foreign Policy." Throughout the book, composed of essays that offer Perkins's own interpretations of what have been the most important forces shaping American foreign policy, he deals with ideas, trends, and interpretations.

IN CONCLUSION

From the literature and trends discussed in this pamphlet we can see that historians and other scholars have begun an adjustment to America's enlarged role in world affairs. That role has stimulated the study of the history of American foreign policy probably more than it has other special fields of American history. With expanded interest have come new ideas, interpretations and even techniques, which have widened and enriched the whole scope of history of American foreign policy. Influenced by world affairs and by new developments in other disciplines, American diplomatic history in the past twenty-five years has changed considerably from what it was in the past, and each new interpretation reflects that change.

If the teacher of American history, whether in the high school or in the college, is to explain to his students the position and responsibilities of the United States in the world, he should know something of the new ideas and interpretations in the literature of the history of American foreign policy. This pamphlet is merely a partial guide. The literature itself is the best source.

www.ingramcontent.com/pod-product-compliance
Lightning Source LLC
Chambersburg PA
CBHW021343290326
41933CB00037B/689